In the Cloud

Poems for a
Technological Age

In the Cloud

Poems for a
Technological Age

Win Treese

CIRRUS PRESS

In the Cloud: Poems for a Technological Age by Win
Treese

Published by Cirrus Press, an imprint of Serissa Research, Inc.

Cover design by Emily Brett.

ISBN: 979-8-9855476-0-3 (ebook)
ISBN: 979-8-9855476-1-0 (print)
Library of Congress Control Number: 2022906858

For Miss Sanders,
who would probably not be surprised.

Contents

Stanza 1

It's Magic

Technology can seem
like magic
but the magic
can disappear.

Maybe
the magic disappears
because we learn how it works.

Often
the magic disappears
because it is commonplace,
receding into the background.

And we forget
about everything it takes
all the human effort
all the ingenuity
all the embedded knowledge
to make our world
full of unrecognized magic.

Putting the Hammer Down

Does a tool
shape the way
we view the world?

They say
for the one who has a hammer
everything looks like a nail.

For the one who has a computer
is the world merely
a problem of data?

Perhaps
there are times
to put down the tools
and see the world anew.

Decoding the Code

Reading code is hard.
Maybe that's why they call it code.
(Not really, but still!)

Where to start?
What comes next?
The computer knows.

We write for an audience.
The audience for code
Is a computer.

Or so we imagine.
But people read code.
Code is for people, too.

Reading code is hard.
Must it be so?
Of course, some knowledge is needed.

If our world is run by code,
Should we not understand it?

Ode to an NFT

An NFT sounds nifty,
The latest techno-thing.
But maybe sort of shifty,
When you find out that it means
A "non-fungible token."

"Fungible" sounds like "fungus"
But it's really all about
Making up a ruckus
With nothing left to doubt.

"Fungible" means things
That can be interchanged.
Put "non" in front—it then implies
That something's not the same.

A token's just a thing you buy
That's almost like money.
But those all can be swapped around
With fungibility.

NFTs are not the same,
They all must be unique.
They represent (what "token" means)
With only one to seek.

First, you mint an NFT
With your crypto-magic key.
Then you put it on the blockchain
For everyone to see.

What's the blockchain? You may ask,
as this starts to get complex.
They say it's like a ledger
That anyone can check.

Then maybe you can sell
Your brand-new NFT
But not the real original
On that we can agree.

If someone reads this poem,
When a few more years are done,
They may wonder what was happening
In twenty twenty-one.

This poem's not an NFT
But maybe it should be.
With its bits recorded perfectly
For all of history.

Why Math?

They say
study math
because it is practical.

They say
study math
because you need it
for finance.

They say
study math
because you need it
for science.

Why not say
study math
because it is
beautiful?

Stanza 2

Reference Points

It's getting harder,
it seems, to write
a contemporary novel
that doesn't feel specific
to a particular year.

What the characters do
with theirs phones,
the slang that they use,
any indication
of what was going on
in the world.

Technology changes.
Language changes.
They pass so quickly,
waves that dissipate
rapidly
even if we
manage to catch them,
a little.

It's easy to forget
the timeless,
or even
that perhaps
we are not that different
from people
thousands of years ago.

Even though
they did not have
smart phones.

Metaphorically Speaking

We did not
think that the universe
worked like clockwork
until after
we invented
clocks.

We did not
speak of analog watches
until after
we invented
the digital.

We did not
say everything is relative
until after
there was a theory
of relativity.

We did not
say the brain
is like a computer
until we made
computers.

We did not
brag of multitasking
until we made computers
do it first.

Could it be
that our conception of nature
is limited
by the technology
we can build?

Pouring Concrete

Poets use the concrete
to evoke the abstract.

Mathematicians use the abstract
to explore the concrete.

Programmers use the abstract
so they can later change the concrete.

Politicians use the abstract
to hide the absence of the concrete.

Some despise the abstract,
getting stuck in the concrete.

When do you use the abstract?
When do you pour the concrete?

Startup 1

You have an idea
for some cool software.

You find a co-founder
and start a company.

You get some investors
to fund the work.

In return, they own
part of your company.

You are excited.
They are excited.

You work very hard.
The investors do other deals.

You ship the product.
Some customers love it.

The investors say
you need more customers.

You pivot
changing the product.

You are excited,
maybe, but not as much.

The investors are excited.
Some early customers are not.

14

The investors say
you need more revenue.

They remind you
every three months.

The revenue is valuable.
What delights the customers is not.

You make a lot of money.
The investors make a lot of money.

The investors are happy.
Are you happy?

You had an idea
for some cool software.

Now it is only
about the money.

One Day

I was in the chorus
of a musical
when I was eleven.

After the first
rehearsal,
it was suggested
that my talents
lay elsewhere.

Since then
I have believed
I cannot sing.

Sometime, in
elementary school,
I learned
I cannot draw.

Decades later,
I found out
that drawing
is a skill
that is learned.

As it turns out,
I can draw, sort of.
Better, if I practice.

I was never told
I was bad at math.
I found it easier
than many classmates.
I was put in the math box.

I wonder
about all the children
and those who have grown
who were told
in words, or otherwise,
they were bad
at singing
or drawing
or math
or something else.

When maybe
they would have mastered it
a day
a week
a month
or a year later.

But a door closed for them
that day.

Stanza 3

The Stories in the Code

A program tells two stories:
one for computers,
one for people.

When the code is good,
those stories are the same.
Though actually, that is not true.

The computer reads
a translated story
encoded into its own binary language.

It follows instructions
one by one, until it is done,
or it keeps going forever.

There is no plot, no arc,
no plan, no revelation
for the computer.

The programmer's job
is to tell the computer
how to get the right answer.

Some programmers
write code only
for the computer.

Great programmers write
an intertwined tale
explaining how and why.

A program tells two stories
whether the programmer
likes it or not.

In the Forest

Most things, we think,
are easier to read
than to write.

Easier to read a novel
than to write one.

Easier to hear a song
than to compose one.

Code is easier to write
than to read.

You know what you want
the computer to do.
You make it do that.

Reading code is like
being amongst dense trees,
a struggle to comprehend
the forest.

Moby Bug

There is a bug
in my code
that I cannot find.

It happens
sometimes
but not always.

When I am lucky,
I know when the bug happens
because my code's answer
is clearly wrong.
Or it crashes.

Sometimes,
you don't even know
there's a bug.

Seeking the bug
can be hard.
The lighting is
not very good.

Once I spent two weeks
searching for a bug.
Someone else had left it there.

It was a single wrong character,
and I missed it myself,
the first time I read that code,
because
I expected it to be correct.

Can writing a poem
help me find a bug?
Sometimes a break
lets the mind work
in a different way.

Coding should make me humble
and more tolerant of others
because my many mistakes
are manifest
so quickly.

Somehow,
that does not happen.

There is a bug
in my code
that I cannot find.

Let Me Count the Ways

Waiting for the school bus
I watched the children play
and began to wonder
as they lined up that day.

In just how many ways
could they arrange themselves
for getting on the bus
like books upon the shelves?

With two kids it is easy
for one child must be first
or the other might begin
if the order is reversed.

It gets a little harder
with three, and we must try
three choices for the first,
two remain—we multiply!

For no matter who begins
there's two ways for the others
And three times two will count them
even if the three are brothers.

There's a glimmer of a pattern
that's beginning to emerge
let's try with four and then we'll see
if our thinking will converge.

Four choices for the first one
and then three more remain
so four times three times two times one
makes twenty-four, it's plain.

And now we know the secret
and we multiply it out
all the numbers from the total
down to one, there is no doubt.

In math this kind of problem
is called a permutation
and factorial's the fancy name
for this simple computation.

That day I watched six children
and I worked it out, no fuss,
that there's seven hundred twenty
ways for them to board the bus!

Stanza 4

Skimming

We skim the cream,
thinking we take what is best.
But the milk still has merit.

We skim the water,
grazing the wave tips,
the feeling of speed.

We skim the scum,
not realizing that the words
originated together
in an ancient word for foam.

We skim the book,
trying to ingest its meaning
quickly,
with less energy.

We skim the code
to understand its function,
trying to avoid
the messy details.

We skim the top,
yet only profit
when we can also understand
the bottom.

We skim by choice,
sometimes forgetting,
sometimes remembering,
that what is left behind
may have value
in its depth.

Complexity is Complicated

Some software systems
are among the most complicated
systems humans have ever made.

Some are complex
because societies are complex,
writing rules and laws
that no one fully understands.
Yet we want computers
that can follow the tax rules.

Some are complex
because they accrete
function upon function,
and no one knows
what it is actually
supposed to do.

Some are complex
because the core was developed
long ago,
and no one dares to touch it
instead adding layers around it
growing like a snowball
rolling down a hill.

Some are complex
because once you let them
get more complicated
than you can understand,
you cannot tell
if it's a little more,
or a lot more,
complicated than you know.

In science, in math,
we strive to find a simplicity
beyond the complexity:
the breakthrough understanding
that lets us grasp the whole.

Software has no
breakthroughs to simplicity.

Simplicity has a cost,
the cost of fewer choices.

Somehow, we usually
want more.

River of News

Some people talk about
a river of news.

They don't say much
about what kind of river
it is.

Perhaps a lazy river
flowing softly
on a hot day?

Or a river surging
through the rapids,
strewn with rocks
and waterfalls?

Or the steady
insistent river,
rarely angry,
always strong,
an irresistible force?

Or the river
swollen by rains
and melting snow,
coursing rapidly,
flowing over its banks?

Or the polluted river
floating with discarded objects
and invisible, toxic chemicals?

Perhaps all these rivers
flow into our daily
river of news,
whether we like it
or not.

Working the Bug List

Sometimes,
you work on the bug list.

Easy ones, hard ones,
have–no–idea–what–they–are–talking–about
                                            ones.

Knocking off the easy ones
is like going for a stroll.

You can report,
"Fixed a lot of bugs today, boss."

Sometimes, you don't want to tackle
the hard ones.

You know the boss doesn't want to hear,
"Still working on that one."

Sometimes, it seems that the company
doesn't care about fixing the bugs.

They only care
about closing the reports.

Water, Ice

Some think of ice
as cold and hard,
of water
giving life.

Yet they are
the same.

Some think of science
as cold and hard,
of poetry
giving life.

Perhaps they are
the same.

Stanza 5

Algorithmic Optimism

My maps app says it's an hour
for going from here over there.
Now I'm late and feeling quite sour,
from believing the mapping software.

I do not quite know how it works.
From experience I'll make a guess.
Using vast swaths of data has perks,
but can still make a heck of a mess.

At each moment the code checks the route
to tell you how long it will take.
The computer never has doubt
in the estimate that it did make.

It changes, of course, as you drive.
That's helpful—it's better to know.
But usually when you arrive,
you feel like you got there too slow.

I think of the map apps as like
an overly optimist friend,
when driving upon the Mass Turnpike
takes longer to get to the end.

So we cannot believe what the app shows,
but really what else can it do?
Would we want any code to disclose
that it's padding the answer for you?

We seem to have high expectations
that algorithms must be precise.
We also want true attestations
which may not be such good advice.

A New Mythology

In the beginning,
they made
digital computers
and thought that
they were good.

On the second day,
the engineers said,
"Let there be wires
to let the computers
communicate."
And they looked upon
their work,
thinking it was cool.

On the third day,
the engineers said,
"Let there be wires
across an entire country,
nay, verily,
the whole world
for the computers
to communicate."
And it was again,
pretty cool.

On the fourth day,
Saint Jon and Saint Paul said
"Let there be .COM and .GOV and
.EDU,
so that we can rid ourselves
of inscribing all the computer names
on this single tablet."
And they smiled, because
keeping track of all those names
was a lot of work.

On the fifth day,
the disciple Timothy said,
"Let there be a web to encompass
the wideness of the whole world,
connecting all of its information."
And there was rejoicing,
because people could show pictures.

On the sixth day,
there arose all manner of
search engines
and online shopping
and social media
and forums
and unseemly content.
And some people wondered,
"What is going on now?"

On the seventh day,
the peoples of the Earth
gazed upon their creation
and they did not rest,
only thinking,
"This isn't what we had in mind."

Amplification

Technology is an amplifier.
It magnifies our efforts.
It lets us go faster than we can run.

Computers are amplifiers.
They can sharpen
how we process information.
To gather it,
sort it,
combine it,
tease it apart,
or magnify our capacity to think.

The Internet
is an amplifier.
We hear voices
unheard before.
We hear the echoing
of voices we like.
We hear voices
we do not want to hear,
though we may disagree
about which ones those are.

Algorithms are amplifiers,
choosing what messages to pass on.

We are also amplifiers
for ideas.
What we say,
how we say it,
who we say it to.

Amplification comes from
choices.
We can choose
what we amplify,
when we talk to
a stranger,
or a friend,
or write on the Internet,
or write an algorithm,
or collect data
for an algorithm.

Sometimes we make mistakes.
Sometimes the listener interprets
the idea differently.

We can choose not to shirk
the responsibility that comes
with amplification.

Even though we feel like hiding
behind the computer,
behind the Internet,
behind the algorithm.

What we amplify
affects the world.

Startup A

You get a new job
at a software company
with about a hundred people
making interesting software.

You are excited
to work there.
Everyone feels like
they are on a mission.

There's lots to do
the company is growing.
Everyone works hard.
You work hard.

Sales grow,
then sales decline.
There's a layoff,
though you are still there.

You work extra hard.
What you are doing
is important.
Isn't it?

The company continues.
The excitement is gone.
You keep working,
now knowing
it's just a job.

Explanations

To explain something
clearly
you should know
more than you are
explaining.

At the edges
of our knowledge
there are gaps,
the parts we
cannot explain.
The parts we
may not have
even considered.

To explain
is to pull back
from the edges
to accept the boundaries
of what we truly understand.

Teaching
is not all explaining.
Much of it
is helping students
explore,
finding the edges
of what they understand,
then pushing beyond.

Poetry
is not explaining.
We can journey to the edges
the frontiers
the limits,
gazing
at the stars
at the mountains
at the sea
or into the abyss
together.

Stanza 6

The Newspaper

I read the news today,
oh, boy.

I used to read the newspaper
turning almost every page
glancing at the headlines
reading what seemed interesting,
even the sports section.

One time,
now long ago,
I thought it would be nice
for computers to make
a personal newspaper.

Mostly, I think
because I did not care much
about sports
or the stock market pages.

When I finished the paper,
I had my news for the day.
It was enough.

I did not know everything
happening in the world.
I did not read
every word in the paper.

I had a sense of what was
going on.
The day's news in the paper
came to an end.
It was enough.

Now the news flows like water
trickling, gushing, streaming
seeping through everything.

Within the torrent
is the repetition
the news stories
I have already seen.

I do not need
to see them again.

I liked the time
when I could
finish the news.

Checking the Mail

I'd like to remember
a happier time
with warm exchanges
of personal letters
over email.

That is never
what I find
in my inbox.

Sometimes
there is nothing there
and I feel
vaguely disappointed,
as if I missed something.

Sometimes
there are many messages
telling me to buy something,
or informing me
of things I already know,
or asking me
to do something.

I try to resist
the beckoning
to check it again
to check it now
postponing the challenge
of writing another line.

I tell myself
there are things
I do not need to know.
At least not now.

I remind myself
my experience shows
nothing good
comes in email.

In the Surf

Does anyone surf
the web anymore?

Or is it all
doomscrolling?

The web no longer seems
much like a web:
interconnected,
related,
linked,
surprising.

Today it seems
like a one-lane road
with an occasional turn
to another one-lanc road.
Each of them full of echoes
of what has been seen
before.

Like a video game
the roads are filled
with obstacles
to the mind
shocking
but not really
surprising.

Or with momentary
amusements
to share with
a few hundred
close friends.

Maybe
surfing was not so great.
Maybe
it was just waiting
for the spider.

I Wrote This All By Myself

I wrote this poem
all by myself.

Sitting here alone
in the room.

Before I started writing,
I made coffee myself.

Well, I ground the coffee beans
and I brewed the coffee.

My team grew the plants,
harvested the beans,
transported them from Africa,
roasted them,
and staffed the register
at the shop,
where I bought them
myself.

My team made the concrete
and the asphalt
that other members of my team
used to pave the roads
that I drove on
to the coffee shop,
myself.

My team made this chair
that I sit in to write
using a laptop computer designed
by other members of my team
and manufactured by
still others.
I sit in the chair and type
by myself.

My team taught me to read
and to write
and other things I know.
I can use those skills
when I take credit
for doing things
myself.

Or maybe
this is not a solitary effort.
Maybe
I did not write this poem
by myself.
Maybe
I really do nothing
all by myself.

If you are reading this,
I think you are on my team now.

For everyone in the world
on my team,
thank you.

I will try
to be on your team, too.

Stanza 7

My Ebooks Have No Shelves

My ebooks have no shelves,
no visibility,
as I walk by
or gaze across the room.

My ebooks do not lure me
as I spy the cover
while looking for
something else.

My ebooks do not taunt me
from the shelves,
reminding me
I have not yet read them.

My ebooks have no heft
no presence
no sensual distinction
no physical aesthetics.

Mostly,
I forget I have them.

The Internet Has No Holidays

Today
where I live
is a holiday
honoring those who died
fighting in wars.

A holiday
sets aside some time
from the routine of life
for rest
for reflection
for community.

Not everyone
gets to have
this holiday.

The Internet
has no holidays.
Always on,
Always abuzz,
Always connected.

Somehow
taking a rest
from the Internet
became a deliberate
effort of will.

I feel I cannot
taking a holiday
from the Internet
for it seems
that no one else does.

Old Code

Old code stays around
because it works.

Old code lingers
because no one is quite sure
how to replace it.

Old code persists
because it is reliable
it has not failed us.
Yet.

Old code still runs
on newer computers
built to pretend to
be the old computers
from when the code was new.

Old code endures
running on newer machines
pretending to be older machines
that pretend to be even older machines.
Such pretension is the price
of keeping the old code.

Old code remains
because we are afraid
to touch it
lest it collapse
like a stack of blocks
when one too many blocks is removed.
Perhaps pulling one more out is safe,
but we do not know.

Old code survives
when there are few left
who can read it.

No one wants to learn it
because no one values it
until critical systems
running the old code
die.

Lost in the Woods

Starting to write something new,
I feel like I am standing on a hill,
looking towards the hazy mountains
in the distance.

Starting to write something new,
I set off down the hill.
This is easy,
I think.

Even the forest
is pretty at first
with interesting rocks and trees
and unworn paths.

I look up
and I cannot see the mountain.
I did not know where the path would be.
Maybe I am not on it.

The effort so far
is tiring.
I feel I must
simply push on.

Am I lost in these woods?
Can I get out?
Why did I do this?
I cannot stop.

I take a break
and rest,
worrying that the break
will be forever.

I climb a tree,
and I can see the mountain
I was aiming for,
sort of.

I see another mountain
maybe a better one?
Or not.
I do not know.

Back on the ground,
I take up my backpack
with all I have collected so far
and trudge on.

Stanza 8

Information Places

I go into the library.

I go onto the net.

The library looks ordered,
with inviting places to sit,
books arranged on shelves,
shelves arranged in long rows.

The net lets me search
or jump around
following links from here
to there.

In the library, I find
related items
near each other,
more or less.

On the net, I am
always in the middle of things,
never at the beginning
or the end.

In the library,
I gain a sense
of the breadth of a topic
and its depth.

On the net,
I have a sense
that I can drill down
following links forever.

In the library,
I feel surrounded
by knowledge and wisdom
that can be attained.

On the net
I find myself wondering
if knowledge and wisdom
really exist.

I find contemplation in the library.
I feel caught in the net.

Rearranging

Many years ago,
after I quit a job,
I wanted some space
on my shelves
for more books.

My wife said,
get rid of some
you don't want to keep.

I did not like that idea.
In the interest of marital harmony,
I began to examine what I had.

Maybe a couple
I no longer wanted
even though at one time
I desired them.

Others began to feel
out of place
like they no longer
belonged on the shelves in my study.

Soon all of the books
on all of the shelves
in the room
were on the floor, or the desk, or the
                                        chairs.

Slowly I put them back
regrouped, perhaps
perhaps in new places
sorting them anew.

In days, or weeks,
or a month,
I can't remember
it was finished.

They were the same books
more or less
yet somehow now
with new purposes, new messages.

Explorations I wanted to make,
subjects I wanted to learn,
books I wanted to write.
Something had changed.

Surrounded by shelves
I looked at them, realizing
that in rearranging my books
I was rearranging my mind.

Entombed Knowledge

Humans are good
at outsourcing
what we know.

Spouses remember things
so we don't have to.

We build systems
each person playing a part
no one knowing
how to do everything.

We construct machines
building in our knowledge.

Later, no one knows
how
or why
they actually work.

Startup Alpha

You have a cool idea
for some software,
so you build it.

Some people like it,
and they want to buy it,
so you sell it them.

They tell some friends
who buy it also,
and maybe tell their friends.

You get busier,
needing some help,
and hire two or three.

Time passes.
Sales grow steadily
but not very fast.

You can spend time
with family and friends
or take a vacation.

Investors notice.
They want to buy in
and scale it up.

You thank them
politely
and decline.

As they leave,
you hear them mutter,
It's just a lifestyle business.

You ponder their words,
wondering,
what's so bad about that?

Too Much Infinity

I heard someone say
It seems like
there's too much infinity.

As if simple
infinity
was not already
too much.

Yet somehow
I know what she means.

There's the infinity
we feel like
we can put in a box
not worrying about it
too much.

And there's the infinity
that is overwhelming
incomprehensible
overpowering
inexplicable.

It turns out
math has more than one
infinity.

One is the kind
that can be counted
if you go on
forever.

One is a kind that
cannot be counted
even if it's
only all the real numbers
between zero and one.

Mathematicians
have found many ways
to deal with infinities.

And yet
sometimes
it feels
like there is
too much infinity.

Stanza 9

Who Knows

Who knows
when I read
the front page
of the New York Times
on the web?

The Times does,
of course.
I expect that.

My ISP knows
because they can see
where the packets are going
even if the data
is encrypted.

Advertisers
and their enablers
know:
Amazon
and Google
and Oracle
and Yahoo
and more.

Advertising technologies.
Companies whose names
we do not recognize.
They know.

Web performance analysts.
Companies we never hear about.
They know.

Companies who promise the Times
to monitor and optimize
their content
for long-term
audience loyalty.
They know.

All this,
before I have read
a single article.

Which also
they know.

Caution: Data Collection Ahead

There are three laws
of data collection.

One.
If data is collected,
it will be stored.

Two.
If data is stored,
it will be used
in a way
not expected.

Three.
Stored data
will leak.

Giving a Reference

When my web browser
requests a page
it tells the server
a few things
about itself.

These things were designed
in the early days of the web
to be helpful
and to make things work
better.

Some tell the server
what human language
and what data formats
I want.

One tells the server
about my browser
who made it
what version it is
what kind of computer
I have.

In theory, this helps
and the server can
send data
that my browser will
understand.

But because some servers
tried to make things better
for certain browsers,
web browsers say things
that are,
strictly speaking,
not true.

Now, there is so much packed
in a little data
that servers infer things
about you
from what browser and
computer you use.

There is also Referer,
a misspelling
from the early days
of the web.

Referer tells
the server
what page
you are coming from.

Servers like to know this.
I am not sure
I like them to know.

In the Cloud

I look up and see the clouds.
Is my data in the cloud?

I look up and see the wispy cirrus clouds.
Is my data scattered in the wisps?

I look up and see the fluffy cumulus clouds.
Is my data in the shape of a duck?

I look up at the clear blue sky.
Is my data gone?

They tell me my data is in the cloud.
They tell me my data is safe.

I look up and I do not know
what data is in the cloud.

My data in the cloud
is somewhere on the net.

Where are the clouds?
Where on the net?

I look up and watch the clouds
slowly float away.

Acknowledgments

This collection is the outcome of a session in the Writing in Community online program. It feels like everyone in the program helped make this happen, especially Akemi Sagawa, Deb Moller, Domenic Chiarella, Janis Farmer, Joann Malone, Marissa DiSimone, Reagan Pugh, Taylor Lilley, and Wendy Coad. Most especially, I thank Galina Tachieva, who challenged me to explain some technical prose with a poem.

Fellow writers Sheryl Roberts, Ellen Mandel, Connie Burgess, Joan Piergrossi, and Maureen Hines critiqued early drafts of some of these pieces. Thanks to Suzanne Summer, Dennis Hahn, Connie Burgess, Jim Fulton, and Tony Loftis for reading an unexpected collection.

I could not have done this without the support of my wife Marie and our daughters Erica, Nina, and Julia. I cannot thank you enough.

The "laws" in "Caution: Data Collection Ahead" originally appeared in non-poetic form in 2005 in my column in *Networker* magazine, published by the Association for Computing Machinery.

About the author

Win Treese is a software consultant and writer. He is co-author of the book *Designing Systems for Internet Commerce* and wrote a long-time column in *Networker* magazine, published by the Association for Computing Machinery. He lives outside Boston, Massachusetts.

www.ingramcontent.com/pod-product-compliance
Lightning Source LLC
Chambersburg PA
CBHW020328130626
46549CB00003B/1066